REALM

of the
CHEETAH

**Survival Hints for the
Beginning Street Motorcycle Rider**

Jim "Barney" Barnett

ISBN: 1491207795
ISBN-13: 9781491207796
Library of Congress Control Number: 2013913708
CreateSpace Independent Publishing Platform,
North Charleston, South Carolina

About the Author:

Jim "Barney" Barnett has been riding motorcycles for over forty of his fifty-odd years. His first attempt at riding was on a friend's 3 h.p. "Taco" mini-bike at age nine. That was the spark that ignited the fire within. He started riding with friends from school at age twelve. Soon after, he acquired his first *real* motorcycle: a 1970 Kawasaki G3-SS, with ninety c.c.'s of raw, 2-stroke power.

Since that time the author has sampled many different facets of the motorcycling community: dirt and street riding, amateur racing, enduro, moto-cross, desert racing, trials and road racing (he's too chicken for flat track and speedway; he would *love* to be the "monkey" on a side-hack, though). Although a fan of any two-wheeled, self-propelled mode of transportation, the author is particularly interested in "older" bikes. His oldest is a 1932 Indian "Chief" project and his "newest" is a 1987 Honda XR-250R.

This interest led to his being a co-founder and charter president of the Southern Arizona Vintage Motorcycle Enthusiasts (S.A.V.M.E.) Region of the Antique Automobile Club of America, in Tucson. The Region produced motorcycle shows/exhibitions and parts swap meets for over ten years. It was a great group while it lasted.

Jim attended his first Motorcycle Safety Foundation (MSF) course in San Diego, back in 1986. The information that he received left such a great impression that the author became a MSF Rider Coach in 2002. He has since been teaching Introduction to Motorcycling, Basic and Confident Rider Courses[1], and provides private instruction through T.E.A.M. Arizona Motorcyclist Training Centers. His observations on the training range, and his desire to help fellow riders, are the reasons that this book was published.

---

1 Trade-mark Motorcycle Safety Foundation

Disclaimer:

Although the author is a certified MSF Rider Coach and teaches through T.E.A.M. Arizona, this does not mean that this book is endorsed by, nor taught as part of the curriculum through either party. The information contained in this book is consistent with instruction of the MSF Basic Rider Course. It is full of helpful hints on how to achieve the course objectives. As the author can not possibly be with every reader on every ride, there is no way possible that the author can verify that the reader/rider is correctly doing as instructed. Therefore, the author cannot be held liable for any crashes, collisions, bail-offs, injuries, nor even (shudder) deaths either caused or effected by or on any reader of this book.

Dedication:

How do you dedicate a work that is a passion in your life, and more importantly, to whom do you dedicate it? Well,... since motorcycles are such a large part of my life, how about dedicating it to those who gave me life?

This book is dedicated to my mother, Lily, with eternal gratitude for teaching me that life is too short to be normal, although she never really said it in those exact words. It is also for my father, Ray, for teaching me how to face everyday life (both the "ups", and especially the "downs") with head held high. Thanks, "Boss".

This book is for the person who means everything to me in life, my best friend and help-mate Karen. She taught me that two "snuggle-bears" standing side by side are quite formidable when faced with adversities in life. They can also touch each others' hearts in ways no one else could even hope to under-stand. With love eternal.

This dedication could not be complete without a mention of that one bright star in the universe of humanity: My daughter, Tamara, who has taught me that love and hope will always endure. I would also like to include my grandsons, Nico, Malachi and Isaiah. May you have as much fun and adventure in your life as your grandpa has in his. And to my son-in-law Zack, thank you.

Last, but not least, a quick thank you to Ron Arieli, the staff, and all of the Rider Coaches at T.E.A.M. Arizona. I've learned a lot from all of you.

Acknowledgment:

I need to acknowledge the one man that made it all possible. I will forever be in debt to Ted Summerfield; my first MSF Instructor from 1986. When I first met him in class I thought that he had to be the luckiest man alive! He got PAID to teach people how to ride motorcycles. I learned how to "swerve" in that class. Two years later, knowing how to swerve kept my wife from being the rare, but much sought-after, beautiful, wealthy young widow. He is the reason that I do what I do. Thank you, Ted.

Table of Contents

Introduction:

"The Realm of the Cheetah - *Survival Hints for the Beginning Street Motorcycle Rider*", is just that; helpful survival hints gleaned from over forty years of riding, and over ten years of teaching the MSF Basic Rider Course[1]; from the beginning street rider's "new best friend".

The biggest problems that we, as beginning motorcyclists, encounter are not usually caused by others on the road. We are our own worst enemy. It's not by choice. It is our instinct! We are slow, bi-pedal primates who have, in an instant, transformed *metaphorically* into the fastest land mammal out there, the cheetah. Unfortunately, mentally and instinctively we are still that relatively slow moving hunter/gatherer.

The purpose of this book is to teach beginning street riders how to evolve through "thinking like a cheetah" and "practice, practice, practice". Did I mention, "practice"? I meant, "PRACTICE".

Here is the first, and most likely, the best helpful hint.

---

1 TM – Motorcycle Safety Foundation

"No matter how many years you have been riding, if you have not taken a Motorcycle Safety Foundation Course in the past, DO IT <u>NOW</u>! You will be amazed at what you did not know, that you did not know".

Nothing can compare to personalized, hands-on training! How can you go wrong with such sage advice? So kick back, relax and enjoy the book. Visualize using the book's helpful hints as if you were actually riding your bike. Then practice them in real-time on your motorcycle, as well as any time that we are out for a ride. If you ever get to the point where you think that you have learned all there is to learn about riding, please do one of two things. Either sell your bike and stop riding, or fill out your organ donor card. I'm getting older and may need spare parts in the future.

Enjoy the book.

Chapter 1 - The Realm of the Cheetah:

Human beings are of the species *homo sapien*. A relatively slow, predatory, omnivorous, bi-pedal primate that, in it's "hunter/gatherer" mode, is capable of short bursts of speed of 15 to 20 miles per hour. At a full speed run a human can stop in a relatively short distance, somewhere in the 15 to 20 foot range. For thousands of years (prior to civilization and agriculture) our next meal was visually identified in close proximity, somewhere in the 20 to 25 foot range. Genetically, we humans are predisposed to look at the ground about 25 feet away for food; security; life itself.

Cheetahs are of the species *acinonyx jubatus*. A fast, predatory, carnivorous, quad-pedal feline that can accelerate to 40 mph in 3 strides, and reach 70 mph in just a matter of seconds. Although these bursts of speed are for distances of a couple of hundred yards maximum, it takes some distance to stop. Genetically, cheetahs are predisposed to look out at the horizon. Can you imagine a cheetah running head-long into a giant termite mound at seventy miles per hour? Neither can I.

The Motorcycle Safety Foundation Basic Rider Course teaches a proper body position with an emphasis on the head-and-eyes up, looking towards the horizon. There are many reasons for this. One reason is that we have a better feeling of balance if we are looking out at the horizon. This helps us on take-offs, stops and slow speed maneuvers. A second, and more important, reason to look towards the horizon is that we cover a lot of ground in very little time when we are riding at speed. Just as the cheetah doesn't want to run into the termite mound, we don't want to run into objects in our path either.

A strange transformation occurs when our gluteaus maximus muscles make contact with a motorcycle seat, we morph from human to cheetah in that instant, and we move fast like one too. Unfortunately, we enter the realm of the cheetah with the instincts of a human. This is not the mind-set that promotes fun rides, rather it is more like a stressed out ride with our helmet on fire.

So how do we humans change our instincts to those of a cheetah? Practice, practice and more practice while ***SLOWLY*** extending our comfort zone. What should we practice, you ask. My suggestion is the four skills that riders are evaluated on in the MSF Basic Rider Course; Limited space maneuvers, Hazard avoidance (the Swerve), Quick stop and Negotiating curves. Limited space maneuvers teaches us operational control of the motorcycle while the remaining three skills are life-saving. The head and eyes need to be up with the eyes towards the horizon to be able to do all four skills proficiently. So let's get back to the basics.

Chapter 2 - The Basics of Starting and Stopping:

My job as a Motorcycle Safety Foundation Rider Coach is to teach the MSF Basic Rider Course as my training and the Range Cards[1] dictate. My interest as a beginning rider's "new best friend", is to help the rider learn these things in the least stressful and (for lack of a better phrase) most fun way possible! If I happen to know an easier way to accomplish a task than the approach that you are taking, would you not appreciate me imparting that information to you?

The students retain more information and have less "ground contact" when they are relaxed and having a good time. This state of being is known as the "comfort zone". As long as we are in the comfort zone we can stay focused on developing the cheetah instincts. Once we bust out of the comfort zone our reptilian basic instincts kick in. We go back to being a slow, bi-pedal primate in the realm of the cheetah. BANG! Into the termite mound! So how do we stay in the comfort zone and keep developing our cheetah instincts? Simple,... we get comfortable with the basics.

---

1 Motorcycle Safety Foundation – MSF Range Cards 2005 - 2009

The most basic actions that we can take on a motorcycle are starting off in a forward direction and coming to a stop. There are ways to do this smoothly and with control; and ways to do it that would make a saint swear. The first "action" exercise in the Basic Rider Course (BRC) is using the friction zone[2]. To understand starting off smoothly, we must first understand friction zone. The friction zone is that area of the clutch lever range where the engine starts to transmit power to the rear wheel as the clutch begins to engage, all the way until the clutch lever is fully released and the clutch is fully engaged.

Those of us who have driven a car or truck with a standard transmission were taught to NOT ride the clutch, because we would burn it out. Those of us who learned to use a clutch in a four wheeled vehicle tend to carry this trait with us when we start riding motorcycles. We are wrong from the get-go! The clutch in our motorcycle has the same name, and serves the same function, as the clutch in our car or truck; to deliver power from the engine to the drive wheel(s) via the transmission. That is where the similarity stops.

The clutch in our car or truck is a single plate, stuck in a hot transmission bell-housing, bolted to a hot engine. The is no way to cool it down. If we add friction (heat) to the single plate by "slipping" the clutch, it can over-heat and fail.

---

2 MSF Basic Rider Course Rider Handbook Edition 7.1
   Copyright 2001 – 2009 Motorcycle Safety Foundation

The clutch in our motorcycle, in contrast, is made of multiple plates, usually in an oil bath. It is difficult to over-heat a motorcycle clutch by "slipping" the clutch in the friction zone. In fact, taking off smoothly and performing slow speed turns in a confined area are difficult tasks to perform if we *don't* slip the clutch a bit in the friction zone.

Taking off from a stop

Taking off smoothly from a stop is an action that some people pick up quickly, and others tend to take a while. It all begins with the comfort level.

Beginning riders tend to have elevated anxiety levels when it comes to getting our motorcycles moving down the road. When our anxiety level is up, our eyes tend to go down. We look in front of the front tire, about twenty feet ahead (if that). We are nervous about the possibilities (the bike can rocket ahead, out of control, we can fall, pant-pant, ahhhh!!!), so we look down for security and (subconsciously) a soft spot to land if need be.

To keep our anxiety down, and our eyes up, smooth throttle control is a necessity. Keep the Marlon Brando, ham-fisted, throttle yanking for when you park (to help announce your arrival). The vast majority of our riding will require one quarter to one third throttle at most. We might need half-throttle as we come down the ramp onto the freeway and see that Kenworth or Peterbilt logo over our left

7

shoulder; just to get out and gone. It doesn't hurt to practice smooth, *s-l-o-w* throttle roll-ons and roll-offs before taking off on our ride.

It requires smooth throttle and clutch use to take off in what most people would describe as a "controlled" manner. This is the first place that beginning riders have real anxiety issues. I have seen beginning students try to get the motorcycle moving by releasing the clutch and then applying the throttle. First on, then off, off-on-off-on, causing the bike to lurch and convulse like a kangaroo rat on crack. These students have the fear that, if they give the bike some gas, it will rocket away uncontrollably as soon as they release the clutch. Somehow, no one ever told them that the motorcycle will only go up to a certain speed in first gear; and that speed is usually not too fast.

Another anxiety issue is what I call the "clutch-dump". As soon as the rider feels the clutch start to engage they release the clutch in one swift movement, usually stalling the motorcycle engine. Stalling the bike at an intersection is one of the greatest anxiety producing fears that we have as a beginning street rider.

If you feel like your take-offs are inconsistent, and you stall occasionally at traffic lights, try this technique. I have found it quite useful in helping students remain in their comfort zone while practicing their take-offs.

8

First; set the throttle. Roll on enough throttle to pick up 200 – 400 rpm engine speed and hold the throttle position at that point. Second; while holding the throttle steady, ease the clutch through the friction zone. Take a couple of steps as your momentum increases, placing our feet on the pegs as our clutch fully engages. Because we set our throttle prior to our take-off, we easily pick up speed in preparation for our shift into second gear. Sounds easy, doesn't it? It is. But how do you know that you are easing through the friction zone "properly"? First off, it will feel good. If you don't know what "feeling good" on a take off feels like, then try a method that I have used many times through the years with a great bit of success. Once the throttle is set, ease the clutch out smoothly, using a silent "1-2-3-4-5" count over about a second and a half, as you gently roll on more throttle. This method allows smooth transition through the friction zone, as well as quickly gaining momentum and stability. Static practice (with the motorcycle engine off) is a quick method of getting our timing coordination down pat.

Stopping smoothly

Stopping is one of those essential skills that many beginning riders and (unfortunately) many experienced riders, could use some work on.

Many beginner riders look to their brakes, and in particular their front brake, as if the brakes are their "fail-safe, go-to" device if anything goes wrong (translation: they burst through their comfort zone and went from "cheetah" to "human" in less than a heart-beat). It is at times like these that the brakes become the "wolf-in-sheep's-clothing". Don't get me wrong,... we **NEED** the brakes. We just need to use them **PROPERLY!**

Most of us have overheard some motorcyclist at some time tell a companion how, as he was riding home from work, traffic stopped abruptly in front of him and, "he had to lay the bike down." If you were to ask that individual what actions they committed to "lay it down," they would not be able to tell you.

FACT: Motorcyclists that deliberately put a motorcycle on it's side to avoid a bad crash are Speedway Racers. Reason they do it - Speedway bikes **DO NOT HAVE BRAKES!**

Any college level physics student can prove to you that a motorcycle with tires in contact with asphalt and good working brakes can stop in less distance than a motorcycle sliding down the road on its side. Can we say, "weight transfer" and "coefficient of friction?" Sure, we can.

When the vast majority of riders "lay their bike down," they have no idea how they actually did it. They just heard someone else say that in the past, and it sounds cool. What actually happened is that they "panic" stopped. Panic stops usually occur at the height of an "OH, (insert expletive)"!!! kind of moment. At this point in time our desire to live causes us to GRAB a big handful of front brake in one flashing instant, like a monkey grabbing a branch, not wanting to fall out of the tree. This causes the front tire to lock, causing an (almost) immediate low-side crash. We just laid our bike down.

Some of the best ways to ensure good stops, and avoid bad ones, are pretty simple.

First: Keep your fingers **OFF** of the front brake unless you are mounting the motorcycle, dismounting the motorcycle, or actually using the brakes to slow or stop. It is difficult to operate either the brake or throttle smoothly when we are trying to operate them at the same time. Keep your throttle and braking separate. And when we use the brakes, we use both front and rear *together*. The exceptions being: use *only* the rear brake when the front wheel is turned at slow speeds and when a tire is flat, use the brake of the good tire.

Second: *Squeeze* the front brake, never grab. One of the biggest mistakes that most riders make in an emergency stop situation is to grab the front brake. Grabbing the front brake does not allow for weight transfer to the front wheel and corresponding increase in the coefficient of friction. At least seventy percent of our stopping ability comes from the front brake because of this transfer. I like to help ensure proper weight transfer by suggesting to students that they use a "1-2-3" count over approximately one second, as they squeeze the front brake. This allows for proper weight transfer regardless if the stop is smooth and slow with a gentle squeeze, or frantic and fast with the brake lever squeezed all the way to the throttle. Just remember, that because of the weight transfer, the more we squeeze the front brake, we correspondingly ease on the rear brake to help prevent a rear-wheel skid.

Third: Practice, Practice and then Practice some more. (Sound familiar, yet?) How many riders do you know that actually practice life-saving maneuvers on a regular basis of at least once a month? Chances are your answer was, "Damn few, if any." One of the best pieces of advice that a motorcycle riding "best friend" can give to a new rider is to practice a couple of emergency quick stops every time that you get on your bike and ride. If you are out on a ride and it starts to rain, don't be afraid to practice a quick stop or two in adverse conditions. Just make sure that you get to an area with no traffic before you practice the stops.

Another issue that beginning riders seem to have trouble with is falling over when they come to a stop. This is another problem caused by being a human. We tend to focus in a narrow area directly in our line of sight, although we still have a larger visible area around the periphery.

When a motorcycle rider is coming to a stop they subconsciously pick a stop point and tend to visually lock on it. As they approach the stop point their line of sight continues to drop until, at the stop, they are looking either to the left or right side of the front wheel. Ask them why they looked down at the stop and they either won't know why, or they won't even realize that they did. The easy fix is to practice (sound familiar?) deliberately keeping your eyes on the horizon as you stop, while learning to trust that peripheral vision more. It won't take long before you realize that your field of vision seems to have gotten larger than you remember. The transformation to cheetah has begun.

Chapter 3 - Keeping the Head and Eyes Up:

There was a popular cadence that the drill sergeants used when I joined the army back in the mid-70's, that had the line: "Ain't no sense in looking down; Ain't no discharge on the ground". Keep your head and eyes up, chin held high, and move like you've got a purpose! Great advise from a tough little S.O.B. in a "Smokey Bear" hat.

It is great advise to the motorcyclist as well. Keeping the head and eyes up and looking towards the horizon benefits the motorcycle rider in many ways. First; it helps us maintain our balance. Watch Nik Wallenda walk the high-wire. He DOES NOT LOOK DOWN! In his occupation, that could easily be a death sentence. Guess what?... the same can be said for the biker. We WILL go where we are looking. You look down and you will go down.

How many new riders have you known that have, on occasion, fallen over when they have come to a stop? Probably a few. When we look down at the stop we *very slightly* turn the front wheel in the direction that we look (left or right side of the front wheel). We don't notice the wheel turn until the tires come to a complete stop. At that time the motorcycle's weight tends to go towards that side, and we lose our

15

balance and fall. Save yourself the embarrassment and keep your eyes on the horizon when you stop.

The second reason to look up is that again, we go where we are looking. When we enter a turn on our motorcycles we are supposed to look as far through the turn as possible. That sounds like an easy task, and it is. It is, as long as we are still within our comfort zone. The instant that we pass our comfort zone and enter that, "Oh 'excrement'!" kind of moment, we immediately return to the human instinct and leave the realm of the cheetah. We look over the front wheel and straighten the bike. At that point we either run off the road on a left turn, or run into oncoming traffic on a right turn; neither being a good option. Why do we look over the front wheel? The only reason that I've been able to come up with over the years is that we are looking for a soft spot to land. There isn't one.

The third reason to look up is so that we can see hazards before we get to them. Watch the cheetah and you will realize that they do not look down, especially when they are at speed. Imagine a cheetah looking only 25 feet ahead and traveling at 60+ miles per hour. It will not be a pretty sight when he runs headlong into an acacia tree at that speed. We may not hit an acacia tree, but whatever we hit, we will have the same result. You can see potential hazards farther down the road when you are looking out towards the horizon. That gives you time to plan, which is a far more favorable option than to respond. The MSF teaches riders to use S.E.E. (Search – Evaluate – Execute)[1] as a strategy to ride safely. It is impossible to search ahead if we are not looking up.

Quick summary – If I look up when I ride a motorcycle I will: feel more balanced, go where I want to go, and make a plan for potential hazards, rather than respond to them. I don't know about you, but it all sounds pretty good to me.

---

1 MSF Basic Rider Course Rider Handbook Edition 7.1
   Copyright 2001 – 2009 Motorcycle Safety Foundation

Chapter 4 - Gimme' some Space... and Time

One of the things that we want, as a motorcyclist, is *space*. Motorcycles are a great way to escape the daily grind, and get some private space in an ever-intrusive world. More importantly, we want the space *around* us; space and time.

We all have that "personal space" that we like to keep around us. There is something comforting in keeping the vast majority of people "at arm's length". At our most basic being, this space gives us a sense of security. We can avoid attack by a quick and simple evasive maneuver: jumping back or to the side. We can also counter the attack by leaping towards our aggressor. Personal space makes us feel safe and secure. Our minimum personal space, while stationary, is usually just past arm's length. Our minimum personal space at running speed, is in the neighborhood of 20 to 25 feet; the distance it takes for us to stop. We have been genetically designed through breeding and natural selection to feel a sense of comfort and security with that amount of space around us. That is fine, for a reasonably slow, bi-pedal primate.

We have to adjust our personal safety space now that we have the ability to enter cheetah speeds, thanks to our motorcycles. We can get the feeling of stability and balance at a "quick walk" type of speed, around that 4 to 5 mile-per-hour range. We should be able to stop in about 8 to 10 feet, or less, at that speed. Once we reach 60 miles-per-hour we should be able to stop most modern motorcycles in 130 to 135 feet. Extrapolate this to interstate highway speeds of 75 to 80 mph (you know you press it), and I like to have about 200 feet clear to the front and rear of my motorcycle. That distance, by the way, is under *ideal* conditions. That space increases during low visibility and inclement weather types of situations.

In a nut-shell, we are capable of speeds that have a personal safety zone of 10 to 200+ feet, with an instinctive personal safety zone of 3 to 25 feet. I don't know about you, but I see lots of signs which tell me that this is not a good situation.

"So, Jim", you may ask, "how do I adjust to this new and larger safety zone?" Simple, by using three time zones that the MSF refers to as "Rider Radar.[1]" The first time zone that we are concerned with is a two second *minimum* following distance. If I am out for a ride on a beautiful, sunny day with the temperature in the mid 70's and a humidity around 65%; on clean, dry, fresh pavement; with new, scrubbed-in tires and new brake pads, I want to keep a ***minimum of two seconds*** between me and the vehicle ahead of me. I want more time and space whenever conditions

---

1 MSF Basic Rider Course Rider Handbook Edition 7.1
   Copyright 2001 – 2009 Motorcycle Safety Foundation

are less ideal, which is usually any time that we actually are out on the bike. The reason that we want at least two seconds between us and the vehicle in front of us, is that it gives us the time (and space) required to stop quickly if the need arises. This is due to three components of our actual stopping distance. These three components are: Perception distance; Reaction distance; and Braking distance. The perception distance is the distance we travel from the time our senses pick up the data and our brain tells us to, **"STOP"**! Our reaction distance is how far we travel from our brain telling us to stop, and our hands and feet actually get to the brakes (and clutch and shift lever). The braking distance is how far we travel from the time that we actually start braking (and simultaneously down-shifting to 1st gear) until we actually come to a stop.

A few years ago I read a study that I'd like to use as an anecdotal reference, simply because I can't find a copy at this time, nor can I remember the author. However, the part of the study that I remember most was that our perception/reaction time in our twenty's averaged between ¼ to ½ second; while in our 50's and above our perception/reaction time was ½ to one second, or more. Now that I'm in my mid 50's, I'm really starting to notice the changes that come from a life filled with good stories (reading glasses; bad knees from being a distance runner and a paratrooper in my teens and 20's; those ten extra pounds that just won't go away, etc.). And, I'm going to fight it to my last breath.

We can work on improving our perception/reaction time by going to a family fun/game center and playing something as simple as "Whack-a-Mole", or head to the batting cages. Start at the slowest cage, and when you can hit more that 5 out of ten; move to the next cage. If you make it to the 100 mph cage and are hitting .500, it's time to go to spring training. You could also sign up for a martial arts class. Unless you like getting smacked or thrown around, I guarantee that your perception/reaction time will improve.

We should work on our ability to stop quickly by practicing a few quick stops every time that we take our bike out for a ride. We only need to practice two or three stops, from 20 to 25 mph, in second or third gear. We can practice the stops in an empty area in a parking lot, or on a side street with no traffic. Don't pass up the opportunity to practice quick stops in the rain, if you happen to get caught in it while out riding. Just remember to work into a shorter stop. Don't try to make your first one the shortest.

The more that you practice your stops, the shorter your stopping distance becomes. This improved skill gives you more "space" provided in the two second following distance (time).

The next time zone that we are concerned with is our 4 second immediate path of travel[2]. Four seconds gives us the time and space necessary to stop or swerve, to avoid a vehicle turning across our path. The swerve being two consecutive counter-steers; one to get the motorcycle around the obstacle, the other to return to our path of travel. The best way to utilize the four seconds necessary to brake or swerve, is to have an idea as to which maneuver to make *before* having to make it.

This is achieved by having twelve second, anticipated path of travel[3]. Twelve seconds gives us the time and space to see potential hazards, and plan a course of action. It is far better to act than react. We cover approximately ¼ mile (1,320 feet) in that twelve seconds, while traveling at 65 mph. If we compare the safe riding strategy of S.E.E. (search-evaluate-execute) to Rider Radar and the twelve second path of travel, we can think of the first eight seconds at the "Search and Evaluate" stages, while the remaining four seconds of the immediate path is the "Execute" stage. A quick bit of advice, though – it is not necessary to wait until we are in the four second immediate path to execute our move. It is better to change lanes for visibility six seconds before

---

2 MSF Basic Rider Course Rider Handbook Edition 7.1
   Copyright 2001 – 2009 Motorcycle Safety Foundation

3 MSF Basic Rider Course Rider Handbook Edition 7.1
   Copyright 2001 – 2009 Motorcycle Safety Foundation

we reach an intersection, than to have to swerve around the car that turns left in front of us, because we stayed hidden in the left side of the left lane. The crash scenario illustrated below was one that I witnessed about ten years ago; not long after I became a MSF Rider Coach. It is an excellent example of how we can use Rider Radar to apply the S.E.E. Strategy.

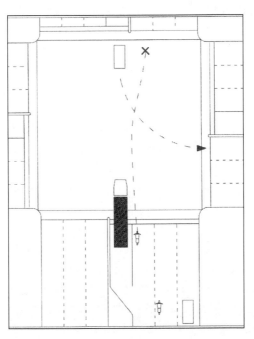

The motorcycle rider in the left lane was hidden from the left-turning car by the tractor-trailer rig in the left turn lane. The author was riding the motorcycle in the center lane, with a pick-up to his right. The on-coming car made the left turn as the rider in the left lane was almost to the cross-walk.

CHAPTER 4 - GIMME' SOME SPACE... AND TIME

The rider tried to swerve and brake simultaneously, resulting in a single vehicle crash. The author had been in the right wheel track of the left lane, but had moved to the center lane because he could not see the left turn lane.

Now that we have a better idea as to our personal safety comfort zone to the front and back, from the cheetah perspective, let's look at the sides. We are limited to our safety comfort zone on the sides due to lane and shoulder widths. The good news is that those vehicles next to us, whether they are traveling in our direction or the opposite, are also regulated by the lanes. Because of lanes and direction of travel, I really don't need a great amount of space to the sides. I may not need it, but I **want** it!

I want to always leave space beside me and my motorcycle. This is my escape route if braking or acceleration are not an option. **NEVER** ride beside another motorcycle in your lane! You lose your ability to swerve in that direction should the necessity arise. This is particularly important to remember when riding in a group. Stagger the riders' positions while maintaining that minimum two second following distance.

So, now we are capable of starting, accelerating, braking and stopping the motorcycle. We know to keep our head and eyes up at all times, as well as how to stop quickly and swerve to avoid hazards. We are very aware of the necessity to keep time and space around us, giving us the ability to Search – Evaluate – Execute, so that we can be proactive to a situation; not reactive. We work on these skills so that we can "Ride to Live" and "Live to Ride".

But, what is it that makes us want to ride these damn-fool contraptions? Are they "cool" (bad-ass, bitchin', etc.); fuel efficient; chick/dude magnets; a quick way to utilize the carpool lane without a passenger,... what? Those are all valid reasons, of sorts. But the *REAL* reason we ride is that feeling that we have when we go through a nice series of curves. That grin that meets somewhere on the back-side of our skulls. The feeling of *FREEDOM*; that feeling of *curves.*

Chapter 5 - Curves, the Reason that We Ride

Curves... the very reason that we ride. There is no feeling that can match the exhilaration of leaning our motorcycle into a curve as we roll on the throttle, sweeping through the turn as we straighten the bike, then exiting the turn under power. Bikers of old referred to this as the "freedom of the wind". If it wasn't for the ability of a motorcycle to lean through a curve, we might as well drive old British sports cars from the '60's and '70's. With the top down, we still get the wind in our hair (for those of us who still have some) as well as room for a passenger, and cup-holders. Since we can't lean a Triumph Spitfire, or MGB, well,... thank Gottlieb Daimler for the motorcycle!

Curves are fun and, being the bi-pedal primates that we are, we love to have fun! If a curve is fun at 25 mph, then it will be more fun at 30, 35, 40... you get the drift.

Unfortunately, that rule is only true up to a point: that point being the edge of our personal comfort zone. Statistics state that 37 percent[1] of motorcycle fatalities are single vehicle crashes, usually in a curve. Simply put, about four out of ten dead motorcyclists

---

1 NHTSA 2005 FARS data

did it to themselves. They went too fast into a curve. Not necessarily too fast for the motorcycle but too fast for their comfort and/or skill level. I have seen people crash in a curve and they never even touched a peg to the ground. They had an OMG moment and went from a cheetah status to a human in less than a heart-beat. That human instinct makes us look over the front wheel for that soft landing spot, which straightens the bike. On left-hand turns we run off of the pavement and into the guard rail. On right-hand turns we cross the center-line and go straight into oncoming traffic.

So,how does one avoid being one of the 37 percent, you may ask. I have a simple solution. Think "slipper" (SLPR); Slow-Look-Press-Roll[2].

Step 1. Slow. Slow the motorcycle to an appropriate entry speed, using both brakes, and down-shifting, if necessary. An appropriate entry speed is one that allows for smooth throttle acceleration through the entire curve. We don't need a lot of acceleration; just enough to set our suspension and power us through the curve. If you haven't been riding long enough to judge that particular speed, then enter the curve at a speed that you would feel comfortable driving your car into. Cars can't lean through the curve, but a motorcycle can;... your speed should be okay.

2 MSF Basic Rider Course Rider Handbook Edition 7.1
   Copyright 2001 – 2009 Motorcycle Safety Foundation

Step 2. Look. Look as far through the curve as you possible can. Surprises on our birthday can be a good thing. Surprises in a curve, while riding our motorcycle, are usually NOT a good thing. If I cannot straighten and stop my motorcycle in the distance that I can see around the curve, then I am going too fast.

Step 3. Press. Press on the handlebar in the direction of the curve. This causes the motorcycle to lean into the turn. The technique is called "counter-steering". Press right to go right; press left to go left. Rather than trying to explain how it works, just have faith that physics does work, and Sir Issac Newton really was a genius.

Step 4. Roll. Roll on the throttle as you press to lean the motorcycle into the turn. You don't need a lot of throttle, just enough to set the suspension and start pushing us through the curve. We can roll on the throttle more, and increase our lean angle when we can see the exit of our curve. We increase our lean angle to apex the corner as our throttle increase works to straighten the bike and "shoot" us out of the turn. This is when the smile generally widens across our face.

Using the SLPR technique to negotiate the curve is only part of the plan. We also have to consider the path-of-travel that we are to take through the curve. We want to set up on the outside of the curve, pressing to the inside apex of the turn, and accelerating out of the curve toward the outside.

The Outside-Inside-Outside path of travel is used because it "straightens out" the curve, reducing our lean angle; plus, it allows us the best opportunity to see further through the turn. To help avoid running wide on the turn exit, it is a good idea to apex the turn once we can see our exit point.

Remember to keep your speed well within your comfort zone when riding the twisties. The temptation to push our ride to the limit is there, big time. Do not give in to the desire to "haul the mail" through the curves. If you feel the need to push your comfort zone, that's great. Just stretch comfort zone under the guidance of an instructor, either through MSF advanced skill training, or any of the fantastic track courses available. Also, check out the "track days" at your local race track. They have instructors available to help you expand you skills in the curves.

Chapter 6 - Keep Your Head in the Game

One of my favorite quotes from the MSF Basic Rider Course manual is,"Riding a motorcycle is more a skill of the eyes and mind, than the hands and feet." We have already learned the importance of keeping the head and eyes up, and why SEE (Search-Evaluate-Execute) is such an integral part of riding safely. SEE becomes much more difficult, if not impossible, if our mental focus is on something other than the immediate task at hand.

There are many things that can affect our mental ability to operate our motorcycle in the best possible manner. We may be tired after a long day; we are distracted by a project at work, or we possibly have problems in our relationships. We may be a bit "fuzzy" after taking medication, either prescription and even over-the-counter remedies. We may even be under the influence of alcohol. All are reasons to keep the bike parked. Let's address each of these topics.

Fatigue is a good reason to not ride our motorcycle for a couple of reasons. First, we have a harder time staying focused when we are tired. Our minds begin to wander and we are easily distracted. Second, we can actually fall asleep in the saddle. Many years ago, a friend in my platoon at Ft. Bragg went home to visit his family in western North Carolina for the weekend. He left on his motorcycle on Friday evening, around 5:30 (oops,... forgot, that's 17:30 hours). He was back at the barracks Sunday night with some bruises and scratches, but no motorcycle. According to Ricky, he was pulling up to a "T" intersection about a mile and a half from his family's farm, some time around 1:00 am. The next thing that he remembered was waking up in the cool, damp grass looking up at the stars. His motorcycle was nearby on it's side, still in gear and idling; lights still on. He said that he had been concentrating so hard to stay awake and focused for the past hour or so, and had started to relax being so near home. He fell asleep coming to the intersection. Do yourself a big favor. Ride when you are rested.

Most of us have enough sense to adhere to the "caution when operating machinery or motor vehicle" label printed on our prescription bottles. And if we are taking an over-the-counter night-time cold remedy, chances are we really don't feel well enough to be out riding our bike. However, we will sometimes take an OTC allergy medication, such as benadrylTM, that can cause some people to experience some slight drowsiness, and then go for a ride. I would not recommend going for a ride if you are one of those people. Do not climb on your motorcycle unless you know beyond any doubt that these products do not adversely affect you in any way.

Also, stay off of your motorcycle if you are trying any new OTC product. Play it safe.

You would think that the topic of alcohol and motorcycles would be a very short discussion, and it should be. Unfortunately, somewhere in the past, the slogan, "bikes, broads, and brews" came into the "biker" vernacular. Bike Nights at the local bars and pubs have become very popular events. ARE YOU (expletive deleted) KIDDING ME? I have absolutely no sympathy at all for someone arrested for DUI. I had an uncle killed by a drunk driver when I was a child, and as a volunteer EMT for a local fire and rescue, I have had the "privilege" of extricating a drunk driver from their car's steering column. It is especially memorable when a family member recognizes the car and stops, just as the deceased is being removed from the vehicle. I think that having to spend a weekend with an ambulance crew should be part of any DUI sentence. Need I say more?

Having said that, I would like to add that I really don't care if you are out on a weekend ride and choose to have a beer and a burger for lunch. Most people take around an hour or so to have lunch on such occasions; the approximate time to metabolize one twelve ounce beer. Plus, you are having it with food and slowing the rate of alcohol absorption. I'm not your mother, and I'm not going to tell you what to do. You are an adult and should be able to make your own decisions and accept the consequences. I do, however, highly recommend NOT drinking and riding. Drinking and driving is a lot different than drinking and riding. You don't have to balance a car.

Although alcohol is a depressant, and affects our motor skill while riding, it's greatest (or should I say worst) characteristic is it's ability to affect our judgment. We relax, lower our inhibitions, and think that we are better-stronger-smarter-faster than we really are. Alcohol is involved in almost half of the fatal motorcycle crashes. Of those, only 1 out of 3 were at or above the legal limit. How about play it safe and just not drink until after your bike is put away? Avoid the hassle and pain.

Now that we are aware of what can affect our ability to think clearly on a motorcycle, let's look at different ways to improve our clarity of thought while out on two wheels. We know that we need to have the ability to think clearly when we ride, but what are we thinking about? As a beginning rider in the MSF Basic Rider Course, we learned that we had to search for potential hazards, evaluate the situation (what-if?), and execute our plan of action. But how did we gain that knowledge? We weren't born with it,... and I highly doubt that it arrived in our cerebral cortex through osmosis. We had to have someone with that knowledge *share* it with us. We had to be taught!

As beginning riders we all had basic skills (some more basic than others), and over time, we improved on these skills if through no other means than repetition. Too often, unfortunately, that is where most riders' skills end. They may ride for ten, fifteen, or more years, but they never seek out further instruction. And they feel that, because they have ridden for so many years, there is little that they could learn. The fragile, knuckle-dragging, chest-thumping, neanderthal male ego is where a lot of us guys will let ourselves get into trouble. I have had students in experienced rider courses that I feel reservation about them leaving the training site to ride home, because their skills are so poor. And that is *after* a five hour class. You can tell them how to do something; show them how to do it, and explain why they should do it... but you can't make them do it. And all because of their pride. If you are that damn good, then why did you sign up for the class in the first place? I have learned over the years that offering advice in a class is difficult enough. But offering helpful advice to other riders that you meet on the road is usually met with at least mild irritation, if not total indignation.

When we first learned to ride, whether through a MSF course or having a friend teach us, we were quite amazed at how much we did not know that we did not know.

I am still amazed that, having ridden motorcycles for over forty years, teaching motorcycle safety courses for over ten years, and having attended numerous motorcycle riding/racing courses, that there is still so much more that I can learn. And I am always eager to attend any new course that I can. The more that we learn, the better we get and the more fun we have when we ride. Our time and space safety margin becomes a very comfortable place to keep.

As a final thought on keeping our head in the game: If you feel as though there is nothing left for you to learn about controlling and properly riding a motorcycle, and you have been riding less that 100 years, please do me one small favor. Sell your bike or fill out your organ donor card.

Fill out your organ donor card anyway. Save a life once your own is over. Give the ultimate gift.

Chapter 7 - Enjoy the Ride

Now that we have worked on our skills and we have the right mental attitude, it is time to go out and enjoy the ride. We have honed our skills to a level where we feel comfortable enough in our abilities to brake, swerve, control our speed, and properly negotiate curves. Our mental state is sharp and clear with a laser-beam type focus. Now we have to make sure that our motorcycle and our body are prepared to ride.

First, let's make sure our bike is ready for the ride. The MSF has a wonderful pre-ride inspection that uses the acronym T-CLOCS[1]. We want to check the following before taking our motorcycle out for a ride:

T – Tires and wheels
C – Controls
L – Lights and electrics
O – Oil and other fluids
C – Chassis
S – Stands (side stand and center stand if applicable)

---

1 MSF Basic Rider Course Rider Handbook Edition 7.1
  Copyright 2001 – 2009 Motorcycle Safety Foundation

This inspection takes only a few minutes, and it helps ensure that our motorcycle is in the best condition to take us out on a ride and return us home trouble-free. Don't forget to follow the manufacturer's routine maintenance schedule found in your owner's manual. The scheduled maintenance helps us find small problems while they are relatively inexpensive to fix, before they become big problems with major repair bills.

The maintenance schedule also tells us when to replace parts that are intended to wear out, before they experience failure. Take care of your motorcycle and before you realize it, you will find people complimenting you on having such a neat, classic motorcycle.

Now that our motorcycles are ready, it's time to get ourselves geared-up.

Since we are talking about getting our bikes and ourselves ready to hit the road, let me mention that the two items I will buy the absolute best quality that I can afford are tires and protective gear. The reason being, that the contact patch of the tire on the pavement is the only thing keeping my motorcycle where I want it to be. If that contact patch goes away, the only thing protecting my body in my protective gear.

One of my favorite acronyms is one that Ron Arieli, owner of T.E.A.M. Arizona, uses on a frequent basis. **ATGATT – All The Gear – All The Time**. That gear includes a DOT approved helmet, eye and face protection, motorcycle jacket, full-fingered gloves, long pants, and sturdy, over-the-ankle boots.

Let's start with the primary piece of protective gear... the helmet. Let me start by saying that personally, I don't believe in helmet laws. I feel that, if you are an adult, you should be free to choose, as long as you are responsible for your choices. Having said that, let me also point out that the race track is the safest place in the world to be on a motorcycle. I am racing against comparable riders, on comparable bikes, going in one direction, with no cross-traffic. If I happen to run wide in a corner, or have the front wheel wash out, I have run-off area. I don't hit curbs and fly into parked cars, road signs, landscaping, etcetera. And if I do get injured, the ambulance is out of the pits and headed in my direction about the time I stop sliding. But I can't leave the pits on my bike without having all of my protective gear in place. So, if I have to wear my protective gear in the safest place to be on a motorcycle, why wouldn't I want to wear it while sharing the road with distracted drivers driving 4,000 pound missiles that are capable of death, destruction and mayhem (also known as "mini-vans")?

It goes without saying, that a full-face (full coverage) helmet offers the best protection. However, some people are not comfortable wearing a full-face helmet. An old army buddy that lives in Florida is a prime example. Let's just say that he's "slightly claustrophobic". I have never known anyone who was more happy to step out of a C-130 into the darkness, than Tommy. He wears a ¾ coverage, or open-face, helmet with either goggles (when he's on his bike with the wind-shield), or a clear face-shield (on his bike without the wind-shield). He has *something* to protect his face.

There are certain *brands* of motorcycles whose owners feel that helmets are uncool, and the less, the better. I know... some of us would rather sacrifice comfort for style. I like asking these people if they would take a fast-ball to the face from a major-league baseball pitcher. I generally get a puzzled response concerning what baseballs to the face have to do with motorcycles.

I then regale them with a tale from my past, the subjects of which are me, and a suicidal dove. I was riding on Interstate 8 towards Gila Bend, Arizona at the posted 75 mph. A dove (the approximate size and weight of a baseball, sans wings) flew directly into my upper left chest at a surface speed of about 40 mph. Combining our speeds, making adjustments for the angled path of impact, was like taking a fast-ball to the chest. If the dove was flying just 4 to 5 inches higher, the impact would have been right into my helmeted face.

If I had been wearing no helmet, or a puddin' bowl/half-helmet with no face protection and had a bird hit my face at that speed, well... we have all seen the errant pitch hit the batter in the face. He spins instantly to the ground. As it was, the bird exploded into gore and feathers, and I received one very large bruise that took quite a while to go away. That was with a heavy leather motorcycle jacket with liner, a sweatshirt, flannel shirt and t-shirt. Imagine a summer ride with a mesh jacket, and meeting the same bird.

Okay, so you are a good rider, and nothing like that has ever happened to you, and you expect that it never will. And besides... what are the odds of it happening? It's only happened to me once in 43 years. All it takes is that first time, and we could very well be referring to you in the past tense.

Enough of my soap-box lectures. Like I said before, I'm not your mom. Make your own decision. Just remember that every decision has a price, and we need to be ready to pay when the bill comes due. I had no idea what-so-ever that I would run into that dove when I left my garage that morning. Physics just happened.

Eye and face protection is very important. Without eye protection, we are vulnerable to dust, flying debris, and watering eyes; all of which make seeing very difficult. A face-shield on a full-face helmet gives us the best protection, followed by the ¾ helmet with a face-shield. If I choose to wear sunglasses, they are worn with the face-shield. Otherwise, sun-glasses are not a great choice, as dust and debris can swirl around them, and they can be blown off of our face when we check our blind-spot beside and behind us prior to changing lanes. Whooof! There went your brand new, $200 plus dollar sun-glasses.

It is important to keep our eye and face protection clean and free of scratches. There are numerous products on the market to accomplish this task. Everything from mild soap and water to specialty plastic cleaners and polishes. A favorite of mine is natural furniture wax/polish. Make sure there are NO petrol-chemicals that will damage the plastic! I have found that the household, name-brand polish that I use dissolves dry, crusty bug parts, and provides an anti-static coating so that dust won't stick. It also provides a coating which repels rain and, when it is cold enough that you completely close down the shield, provides a fresh, lemony scent. Much better than stinky helmet "funk". (Hint: don't be afraid to wash your helmet comfort liner once in a while.)

When you choose a motorcycle jacket, make sure that it is actually a "motorcycle" jacket, rather than a Hollywood, wanna-be fashion statement. Motorcycle specific jackets are made for the sole-purpose of being worn while riding. They have a different cut and style to them. They are wider, or billowed at the shoulders, and the sleeves are a bit longer with a slight bend in the elbow area. The back is also cut a bit longer to prevent that cold bubble of air behind us to find its way to our, ahem,... warmer, nether regions accessed via the "plumber" butt-crack. Jackets can be made from leather, or any of the various abrasion-resistant synthetic fabrics.

Most motorcycle jackets have a removable liner, as well as a ventilation system, and high-visibility, reflective piping along the seams.

Our gloves should also be motorcycle specific. While leather work gloves are better than no gloves, it is much better to purchase gloves designed for riding motorcycles. They have their seams away from the palms to avoid bunching and blistering. They also have a natural-shaped curve to help work our controls more effectively. You should wind up with at least two, possibly more, pairs of motorcycle gloves for different seasons and situations. Make sure that your gloves cover the entire finger. Yeah, shorty, finger-less gloves look cool, but until you lose the skin on the end of a finger tip, you don't realize how long it takes for feeling to come back to that area.

Wearing long pants while riding a motorcycle should be basic enough that we shouldn't have to discuss it. But every year we see them; the guy out on his bike, wearing a full-face helmet, a t-shirt, shorts, and sneakers. Here is a news flash, amigo. Shock from sliding down the road and losing large amounts of skin will kill you just as dead as a severe head injury. Dead is dead. Most motorcyclists wear denim jeans when they ride, and that is good. However, wearing chaps or motorcycle over-pants over the denim gives us a whole lot more protection. The only problem that I have found with chaps is that they don't cover the area that I would prefer to be covered when I get caught riding in the rain. You are wet and cold where you would much prefer to be warm and dry.

Finally, we should be wearing sturdy, over-the-ankle boots with a low heel and rubber, oil-resistant soles. We need good ankle support for when we put our foot down at a stop. Hiking or work boots work well, but motorcycle specific boots work better. They have added padding where the shift lever contacts the foot, as well as being easy to put on and remove. A large number of motorcycle boots also have retro-reflective panels near the heel, which aids visibility at night. Make sure that the heel is no more that an inch, to an inch and a half high. Any more heel than that makes it very difficult to properly operate the rear brake and shift lever, as the heel can easily get caught on the foot peg.

Unless you were distracted or not paying attention, you probably noticed that I kept "suggesting" motorcycle specific riding gear. Most companies that produce motorcycle specific clothing and gear provide professional racers with their gear. When a racer becomes separated from his bike and has to use his gear for its intended purpose, they do not throw the crashed-in gear away. That gear goes back to the manufacturer and is disassembled and inspected. They find out what worked and what did not, and they make changes accordingly. It is a reassuring feeling to know that your gear went through R&D in real-life crash scenarios.

CHAPTER 7 - ENJOY THE RIDE

Well, we have learned how important it is to be able to properly operate our motorcycle, and to be able to perform life-saving maneuvers consistently. We understand the importance of keeping our head and eyes up in our never-ending quest to Search-Evaluate-Execute. And we understand the necessity of properly negotiating curves. We have mentally and physically prepared ourselves to ride, and have made sure that our motorcycle is in the best possible condition for our ride. The transformation from human to cheetah has begun in earnest. It is time to go and enjoy the ride.

Closing Comments

This book should not be used as a motorcycle training manual. If you have never taken a motorcycle safety course, my suggestion is to DO IT! Nothing will ever replace personalized instruction. This book is a collection of helpful hints that I've come up with over the years, to help beginning riders grasp the concepts of skills taught in the Basic Rider Course. Those skills, **WHEN PRACTICED**, will help keep us safe while riding. Unfortunately, many students are anxious about their ability to ride. That is when a little absurd humor comes in. The same people who are thinking so much that they can't hear you tell them to look up, will hear you talk about the cheetah and relate. Go figure.

Maybe, on your next ride, something will happen that makes you think about having read this book. Maybe you'll chuckle at the thought of yourself transforming into a cheetah as you sit on the bike; or maybe at the slap-stick humor of the cheetah looking down and bouncing off a termite mound (and your desire to avoid a similar situation). If that happens, and it reminds you to practice the life-saving skills, then this book has served it purpose.

To find a motorcycle safety class in your area contact the Motorcycle Safety Foundation. You can check them out at www.msf-usa.org. Take a course, even if (and especially if) you feel that you don't need one. You might be very surprised.

Have a fun ride, no matter what you ride!